M000017762

Life Lessons

from

CATSASS

Life Lessons
from
CATSASS

CLAUDE COMBACAU

Andrews McMeel
PUBLISHING®

Welcome to my book, human. On the following pages, you will find games, exercises, quizzes, and many other activities. Don't think I mean to entertain you ... My real aim is to show you that the life of a cat is a million times better than yours!

POLITENESS GUIDE

Catsass tips to avoid sounding rude
when saying horrible things to people you despise.

Don't say:

 URH, YOU HAVE SUCH BAD BREATH!

 BUT

 THE SMELL COMING FROM YOUR MOUTH MAKES ME BELIEVE YOU HAD FECES FOR LUNCH.

Don't say:

 WHOA, WHY ARE YOU SO UGLY??

 BUT

HAVE YOU HEARD ABOUT THIS NEW TREND OF WEARING A PAPER BAG OVER YOUR HEAD?

Don't say:

  SHUT THE FUCK UP.

 BUT

 HAVE YOU NOTICED HOW PEACEFUL I LOOK WHEN YOU'RE QUIET?

Cat's ass art

Why do we always have to represent cats' buttholes as stars?
Draw it the way you like. Heart shaped or square shaped . . .
Just express yourself freely!

BUY ME!

Your cat is a junkie

SPEND MONEY ON MAKING KITTY HIGH & WOBBLY

CATNIP

⚠ May contain traces of eggs, milk, nuts, and rodents.

BEAUTY: How to be beach-body ready?

BE A CAT. NO ONE WILL CARE ABOUT YOUR MUFFIN TOP.

SCOOP

CATSASS'S MOST
EMBARRASSING
MOMENTS

LET'S PLAY!

Put the pieces of the $3,000 vase Catsass just destroyed back together.*
Three pieces are parts of other ruined objects. Because you don't deserve to have it easy.

IT WAS WRONG
& I LOVED IT.

*Seriously though, don't do it. It's impossible.

How to become a cat

3-step course:

① Stop shaving

② Make a judgmental face

③ Freak out
when you see a
piece of foil

CROSSWORDS

50 shades of meow

1. When I'm hungry 2. Sound of boredom 3. In case of emergency
4. The true meaning of life 5. Can be used to say hello AND fuck you
6. The song of my people 7. Expression of anger
8. A synonym for "play with me" 9. Indication that you should probably stop talking
10. Getting my tail stepped on

1. Meow 2. Meeooowww 3. Meooow 4. Miimmeoowww 5. Meoow 6. Meeew 7. Miimeow 8. Meeooww 9. Meoo 10. Meooooowww

CATSASS'S BEAUTY ROUTINE

① Wash yourself thoroughly

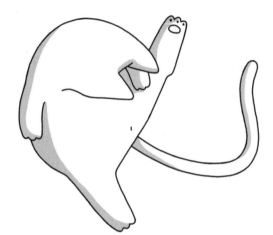

② Don't forget to clean behind your ears and between your toes

③ Roll yourself in litter every once in a while

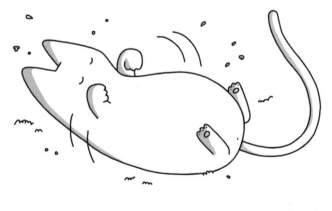

④

Rehydrate yourself as much as you can

Cut on dotted lines

Make kitty talk

DiY

Make your own paper Catsass

Post your pictures on Instagram and tag @catsasss!

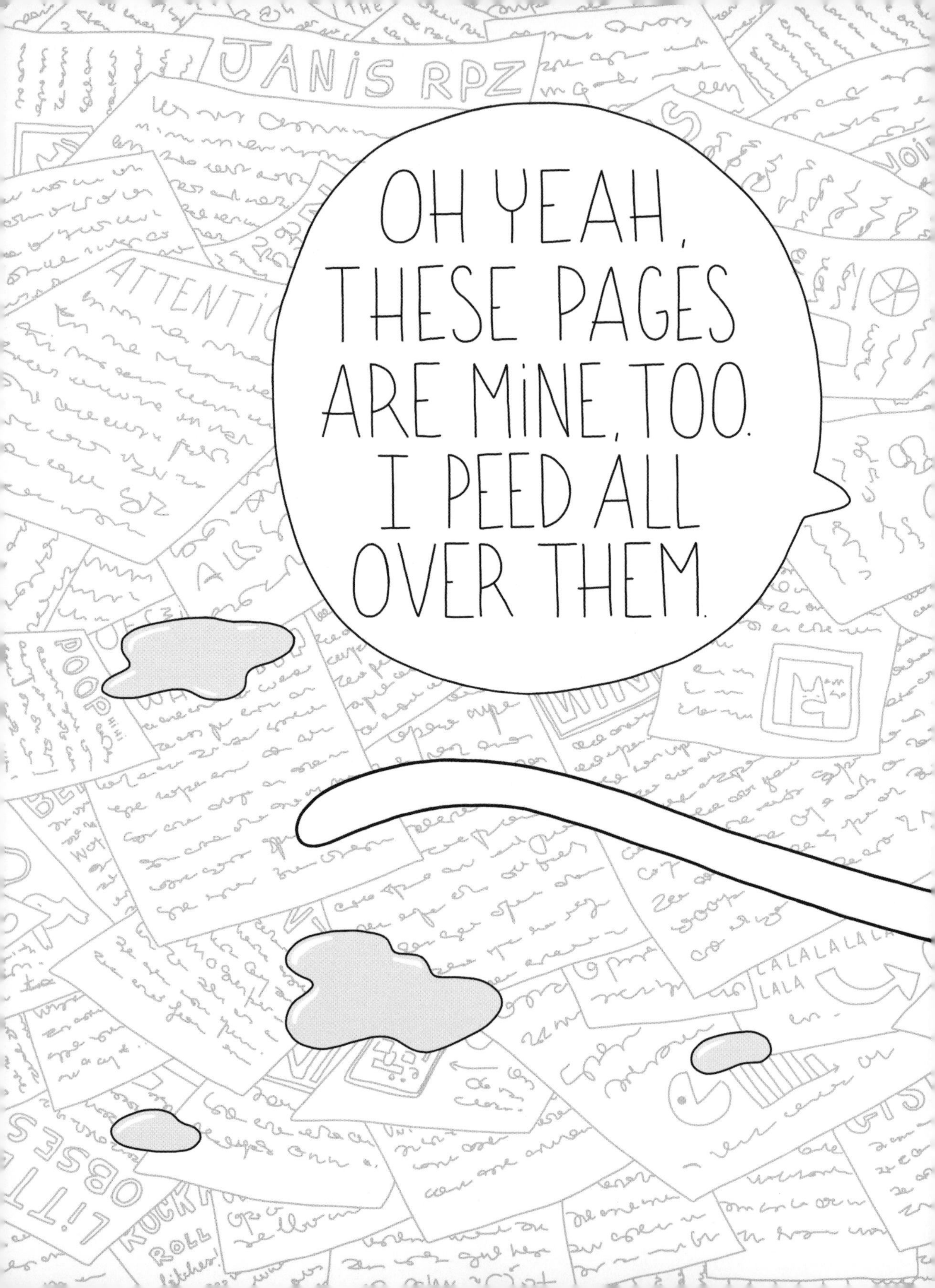
OH YEAH, THESE PAGES ARE MINE, TOO. I PEED ALL OVER THEM.

Micey spicy

Discover Catsass's perfect burger recipe!

Gluten-free
bun.
Cats are
hipsters.

Cheddar cheese,
even if
lactose intolerant.

Wet-food patty.
For meat lovers
who suck
at hunting.

Fish-flavored
sauce.

Stolen sock.
Pretty hard
to digest.

Bacon.
To give life
meaning

Cat equivalent
to pickles:
It's here,
but no one
will ever
eat it.

Lettuce,
for cleansing.

-MEAN CAT SURVIVAL KIT-

Products that should already exist

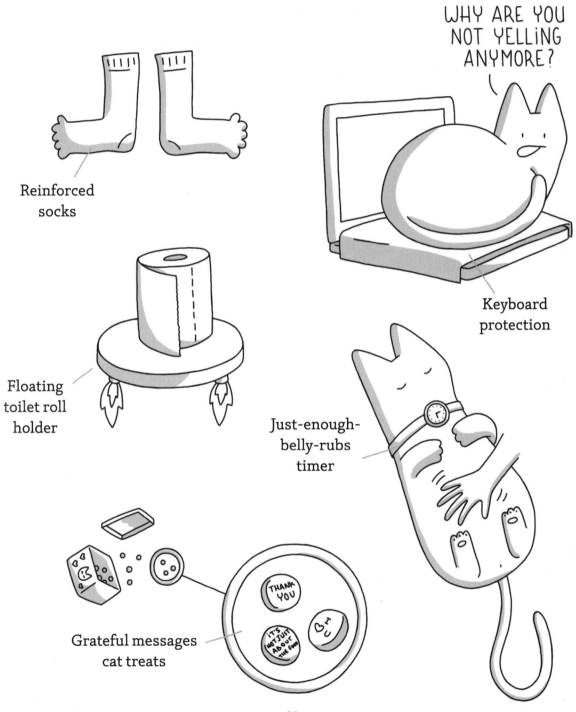

Reinforced socks

Keyboard protection

Floating toilet roll holder

Just-enough-belly-rubs timer

Grateful messages cat treats

FREE EXPRESSION WALL

If you don't understand why cats like ruining furniture and stuff all the time, grab a pen and give it a try here.

WAKE UP!

Help Catsass
find a way to his human's toes

Anatomy of a mean kitty

Tiny ears

Endearing muzzle for telling you how grateful he is

Pink soft cushions

Big lovely eyes

Adorable paws

Fluff everywhere

Delightful belly

Delicate feet

Soft tail for expressing love and affection

COLOR THE TROPHY WALL

Last night's leftovers

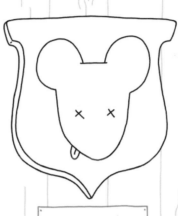

The late plaything

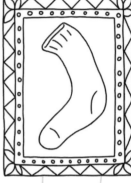

It's not the washing machine that stole your socks

A well-deserved ending

Hairball masterpiece

Annoying buzzing thing

Treasure hunt

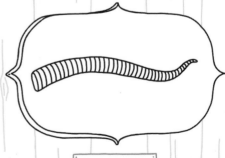

Rodent's tail

CAT LOTTO

1	2	3	4	5
6	7	8	9	10
11	12	13	14	15
16	17	18	19	20
21	22	23	24	25
26	27	28	29	30
31	32	33	34	35
36	37	38	39	40

Get a chance to win the CATSASS LOTTERY! Check 5 boxes, send in your ticket and a $150 admission fee to hellocatsass@gmail.com*

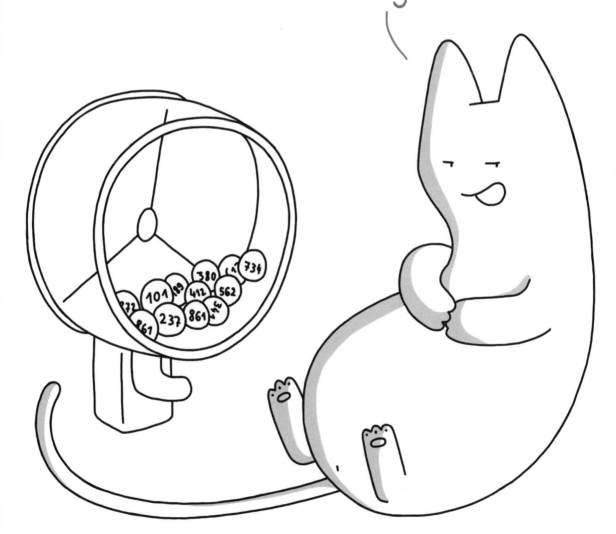

*The editor disclaims all liability in case of a scam, bank account hacking, or gambling addiction.

IN CASE OF AN ALIEN INVASION...

CATS SHOULD DEFINITELY BE IN CHARGE OF THE SITUATION.

Welcome the invaders in a warm, yet intriguing way.

Intimidate them to show who's the boss.

DON'T MESS WITH ME, FLUBBER.

**Show them
the local customs.**

4.

**Distract them
while your accomplices
steal their spaceships.**

Too bad cats
don't have the
best eyesight.

Catsassy faces

Neutral

Annoyed

Sleeping

Sarcastic

Judgmental

Scared

Looking for food

Fed

Asking a favor

Now it's your turn!

TEST: Are you a real cat?

① When you're hungry:

a. You either pick something in the fridge or order food.

b. You roam the floor hoping to find leftovers.

c. You hunt. Ideally a tin can or a piece of turkey on the dinner table.

② If you feel like going outside:

a. You put your shoes on and open the door.

b. You wait peacefully in front of the door until someone puts a leash on you and takes you out.

c. You mew nonstop until the door opens. Preferably around 4 a.m.

③ You would describe your relationship to others as . . .

a. Quite complex; people are hard to understand.

b. Everyone is fantastic, you love people! Except the mailman.

c. Hell is other people.

4) If you were crazy rich, you would . . .

a. Travel around the world, buy a boat and a plane, and party all day.

b. Get a mansion with a HUGE garden and run around with friends all day. And a ball pit.

c. Buy an island in the middle of nowhere, get three mute servants, and sleep.

5) What do you like to do when you are bored?

a. Surf the Internet, play Candy Crush, or watch TV.

b. Follow your own tail or bark at your own farts.

c. Pretend you are simply looking at the wall when you are actually devising your plan to conquer the world.

Answers

Mostly a. You're some boring human. Just kill yourself. Maybe you'll reincarnate as a cat next time.

Mostly b. You're a dog. How do you even have enough neurons to read this?

Mostly c. Congratulations, you're a cat. Just keep on being awesome.

② FOLD HERE

③ AND HERE

① CUT HERE

DIY KITTY TOY

Why spend a fortune on toys your cat won't play with?
Learn how to make a super awesome game with nothing
but paper and your own two hands!

④ HERE, TOO

⑥ YOU CAN ALSO DECORATE IT. YOUR CAT WON'T CARE, THOUGH.

⑤ WELL, YOU GET THE POINT.

Who needs wrapping paper when you can have A CAT?

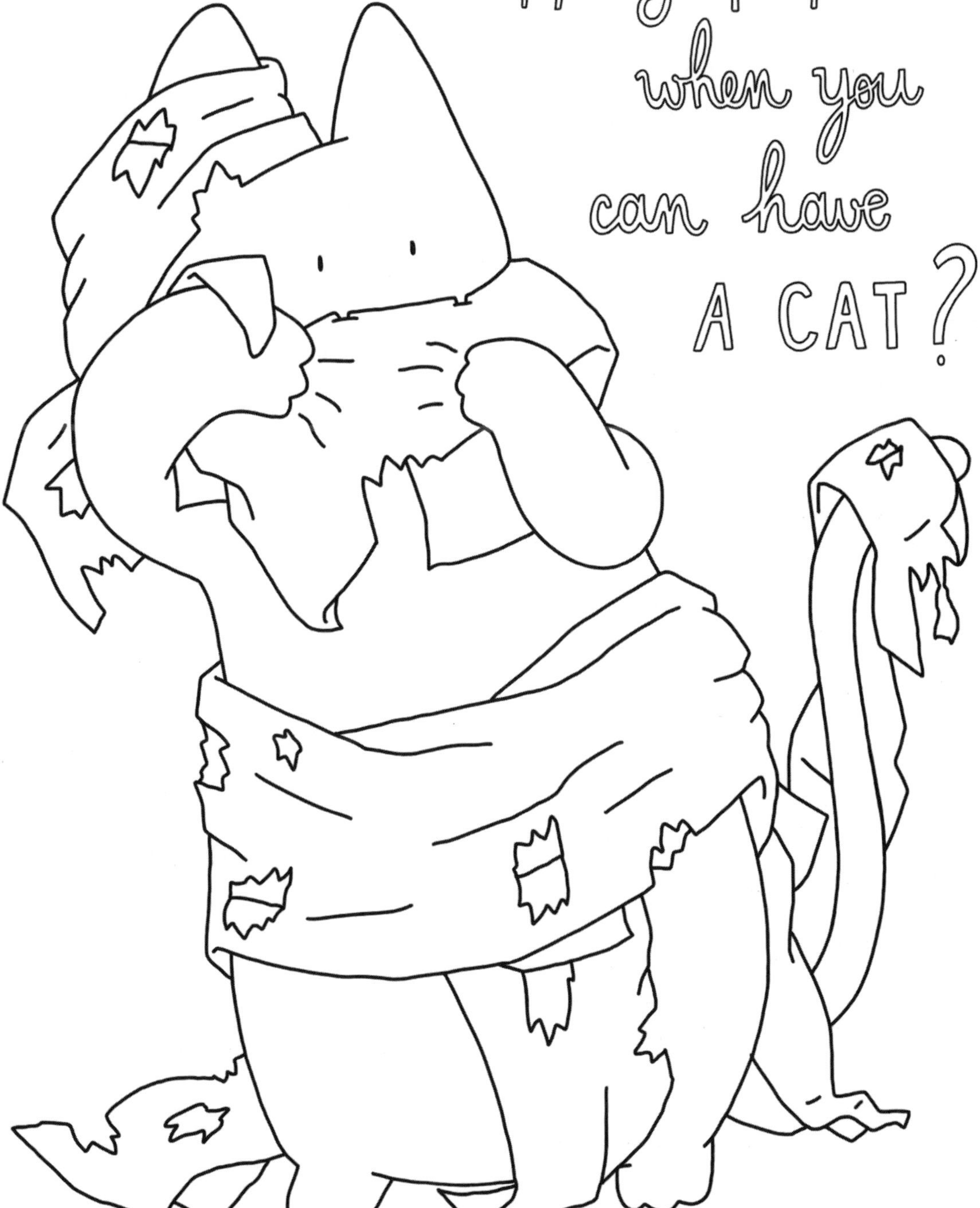

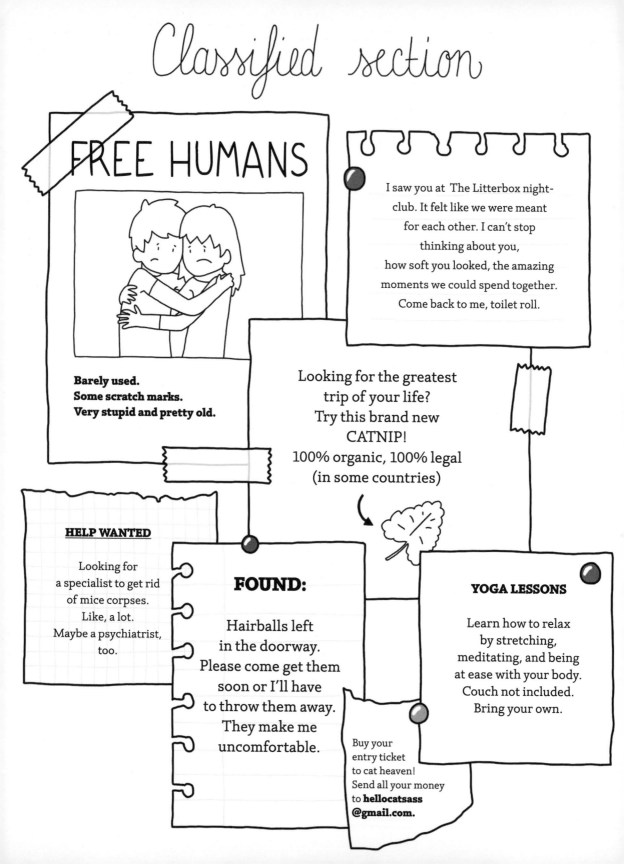

FREE HUMANS

Barely used.
Some scratch marks.
Very stupid and pretty old.

I saw you at The Litterbox nightclub. It felt like we were meant for each other. I can't stop thinking about you, how soft you looked, the amazing moments we could spend together. Come back to me, toilet roll.

Looking for the greatest trip of your life? Try this brand new CATNIP! 100% organic, 100% legal (in some countries)

HELP WANTED

Looking for a specialist to get rid of mice corpses. Like, a lot. Maybe a psychiatrist, too.

FOUND:

Hairballs left in the doorway. Please come get them soon or I'll have to throw them away. They make me uncomfortable.

Buy your entry ticket to cat heaven! Send all your money to **hellocatsass @gmail.com.**

YOGA LESSONS

Learn how to relax by stretching, meditating, and being at ease with your body. Couch not included. Bring your own.

CATSASS PHiLOSOPHY

One day, evolution decided
to make catfish look like this . . .

. . . instead of that.

Life is such a bitch.

Human Remote Control

Take over your biped's mind!

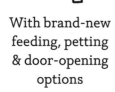

Amazing features!

With brand-new feeding, petting & door-opening options

Does not work with paws.

My life is so much
better than yours ♡

Dear loser,
I'm so busy being awesome
all I could get you was
this ready-made card.

XOXO

CATS ARE FEARLESS

It's certainly not because we're afraid.

So **WHY** do they hate going to the vet so much?

We're not pussies.

It's just that it would be a waste of one of our 9 lives to catch a nosocomial disease.

HAVING A CAT AROUND WHEN YOU'RE SICK

Best idea ever (not).

I don't care if you're too hot. I won't budge.

He keeps you warm.

This soup is gross. Let me eat it for you.

He makes sure you're comfortable.

He cheers you up (by putting things in perspective).

For heaven's sake, stop complaining about your stuffy nose.

Learn how to read the future in kitty's fluffy paw

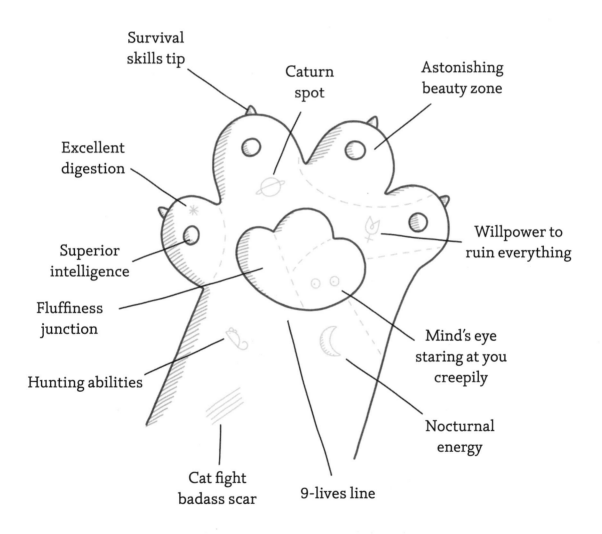

Survival skills tip

Caturn spot

Astonishing beauty zone

Excellent digestion

Superior intelligence

Fluffiness junction

Hunting abilities

Willpower to ruin everything

Mind's eye staring at you creepily

Nocturnal energy

Cat fight badass scar

9-lives line

A brief, 100% accurate look back at feline history

by Prof. Catsass

I wear glasses.
You can trust me.

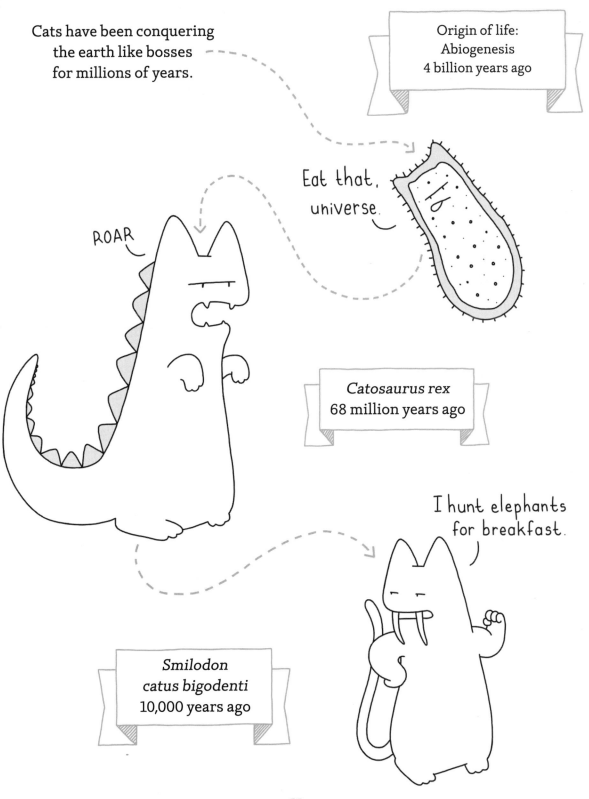

Throughout history, kitties were adored, and humanity understood quickly enough that they were of the highest intellect.

Ancient Egypt: Cats are considered gods.

Deal with it.

Yeah, alright, I caught a mouse. Now bring me real food and scratch my back.

Beginning of so-called "domestication": They help to control the pests.

I am so badass.

Vikings kept cats as companions and rat hunters.

Unfortunately, they also had their dark times . . .

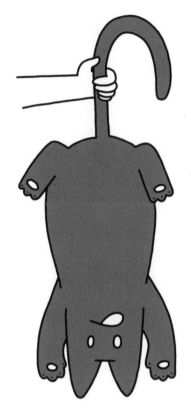

During the Middle Ages cats were associated with superstition and witchcraft. They were considered animals of sin and were thought to be associated with Satan.

What do you mean, "devil's work"? Do you believe in Santa, too ??

That's for bullying my people.

But they got their revenge soon enough, don't worry.

I'm gonna ruin your shoes while you're busy.

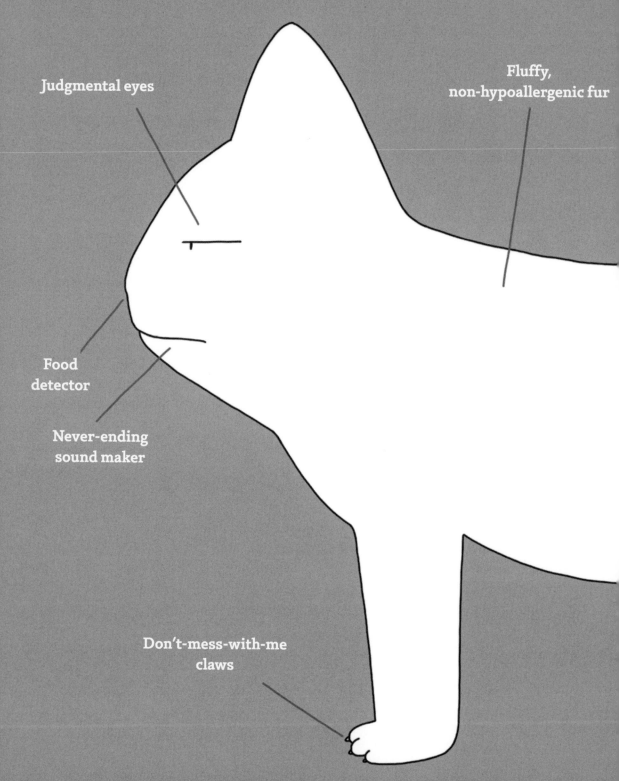

Judgmental eyes

Fluffy,
non-hypoallergenic fur

Food
detector

Never-ending
sound maker

Don't-mess-with-me
claws

ANATOMY OF A MEAN KiTTY

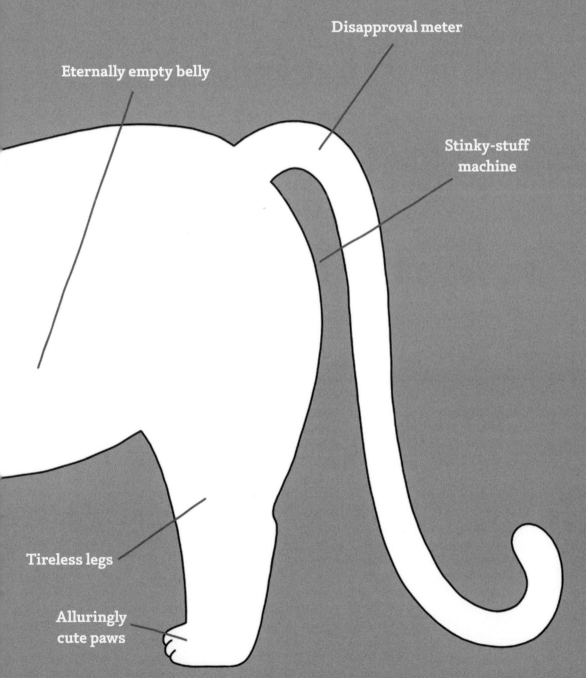

Disapproval meter

Eternally empty belly

Stinky-stuff machine

Tireless legs

Alluringly cute paws

TEST

Is your kitty a real Catsass?

Open the book flat on these pages, and see if he sits on it as a real cat would on a real computer.

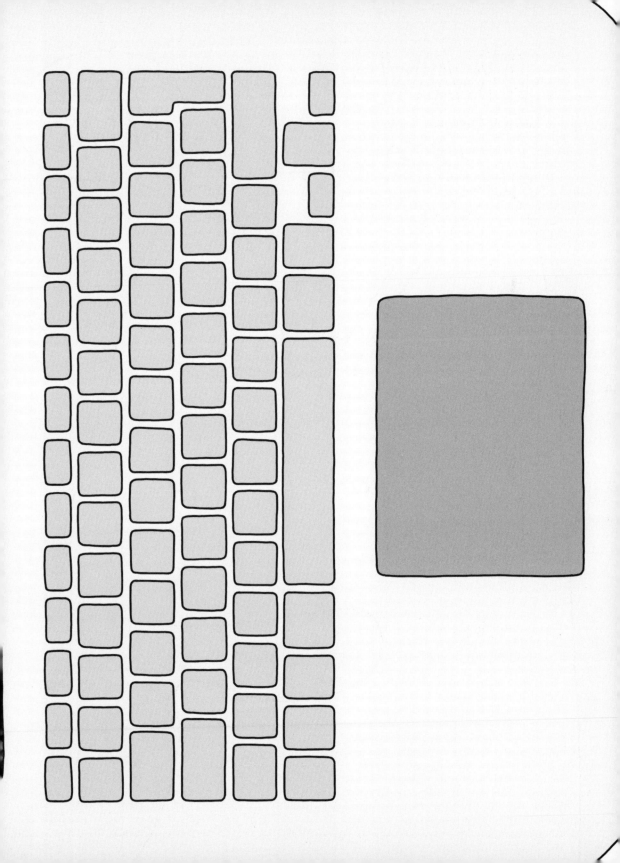

MAKEUP TUTORIAL

Gather the products,
choose the right shades,
and make sure
they fit your skin type.

Throw everything away.

Just be cute and
stop caring.
You're a cat.

Contract

I hereby agree to sell my soul eternally to kitties, especially mine. This agreement also involves interrupting any social or professional activity in case of feline existence of any sort in the surroundings (i.e., mewing, presence of a cat tree, scratched furniture, etc.).
Besides, I undertake to watch cat videos at least three times a day.

Date: Signature:

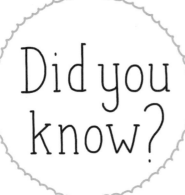

Did you know?

CATS ARE NEARSIGHTED

Which doesn't prevent me from noticing that you look like shit.

KiTTY BODY LANGUAGE

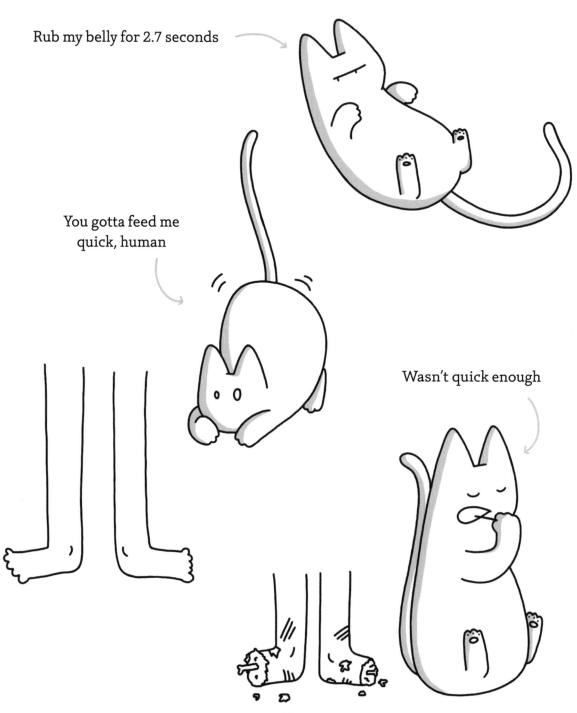

Rub my belly for 2.7 seconds

You gotta feed me quick, human

Wasn't quick enough

Don't get too comfy here

The house needs refurbishing

The curtains didn't
match my eye color

I am globally unhappy
with your behavior, biped

LEARN CATSASS'S POKER MOVES

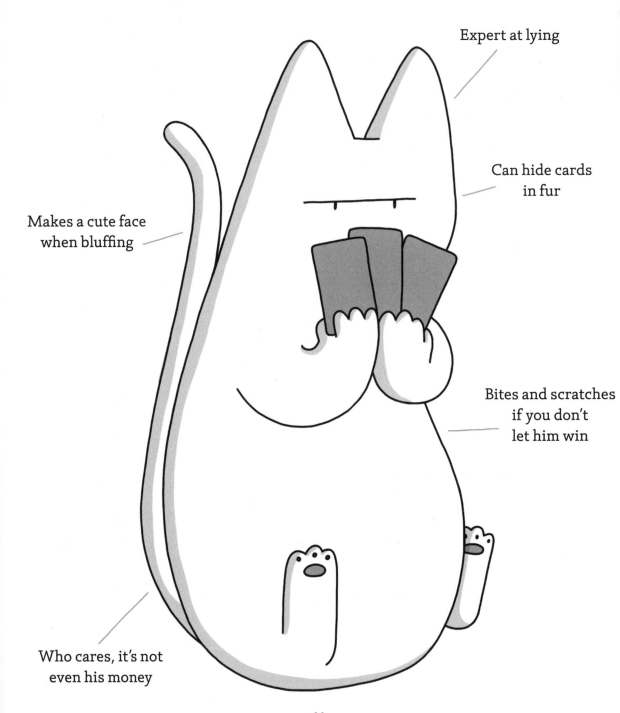

Expert at lying

Can hide cards in fur

Makes a cute face when bluffing

Bites and scratches if you don't let him win

Who cares, it's not even his money

3 REASONS WHY YOU SHOULDN'T TALK ABOUT YOUR CAT

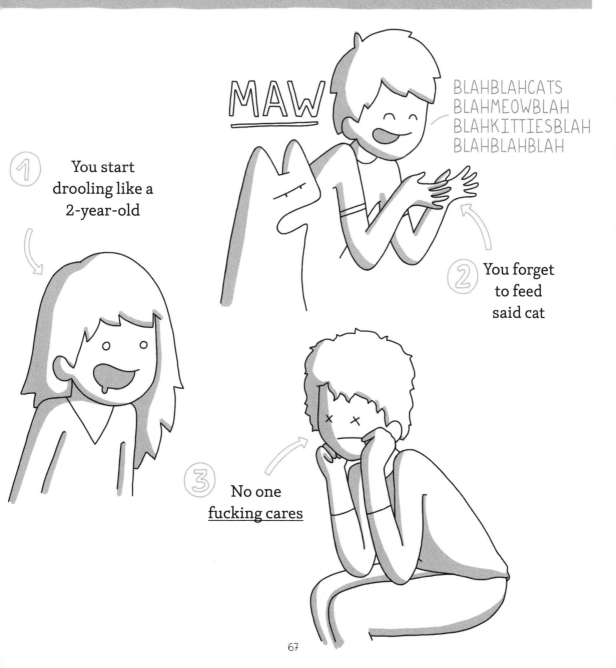

1. You start drooling like a 2-year-old

2. You forget to feed said cat

3. No one fucking cares

GAME ON!

Guess whose lap kitty is going to pick!

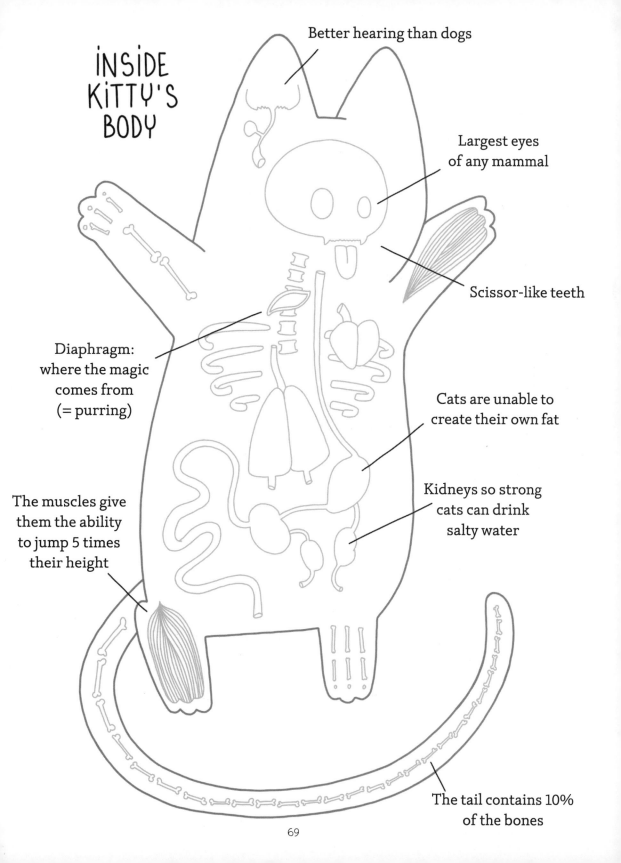

INSIDE KITTY'S BODY

Better hearing than dogs

Largest eyes of any mammal

Scissor-like teeth

Diaphragm: where the magic comes from (= purring)

Cats are unable to create their own fat

Kidneys so strong cats can drink salty water

The muscles give them the ability to jump 5 times their height

The tail contains 10% of the bones

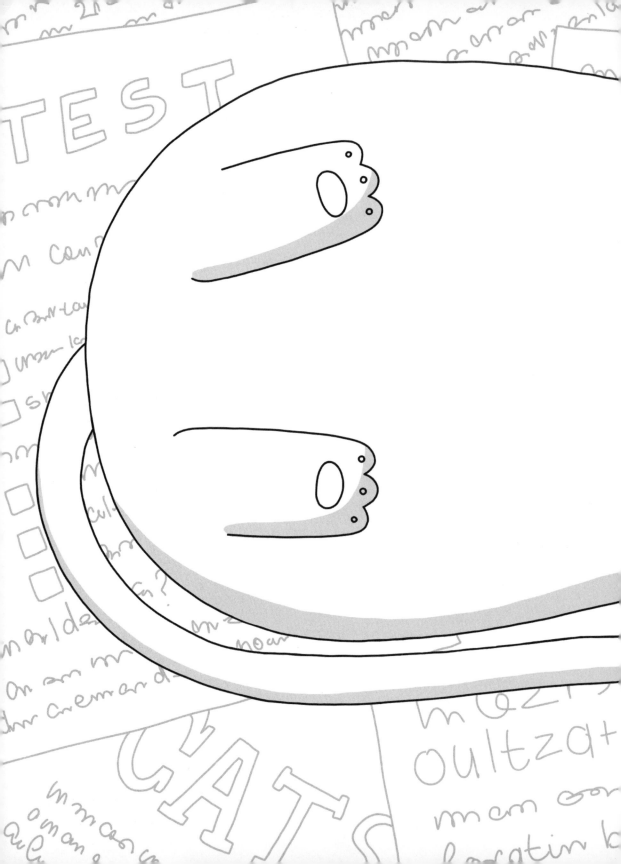

Catsass's birthday cake recipe

① Preheat the oven and sit next to it
for at least 2 hours

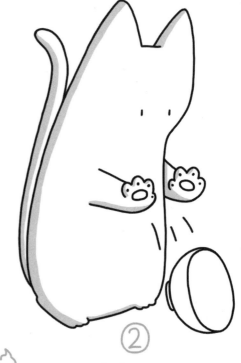

② Push the mixing
bowls over

③ Roll yourself in flour

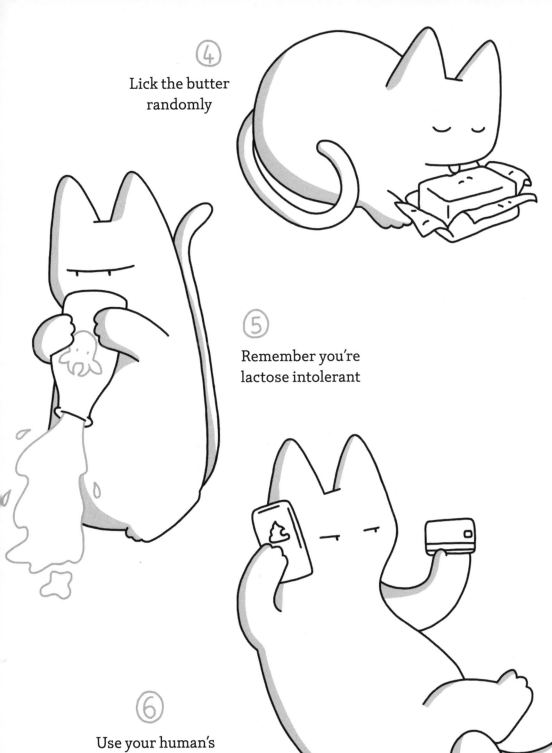

④ Lick the butter randomly

⑤ Remember you're lactose intolerant

⑥ Use your human's credit card to buy one. Not the cheap kind.

KiTTY DANCE MOVES!

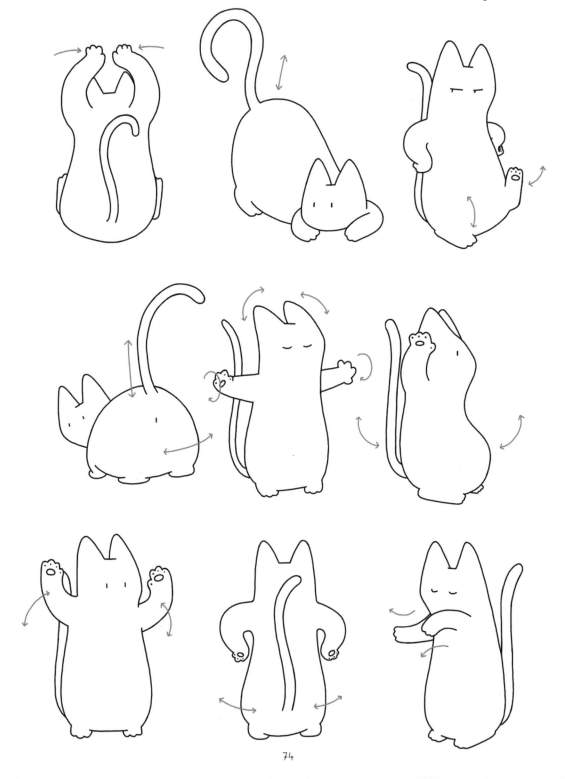

Connect the dots to see
the message Catsass
is sending with
the laser pointer!

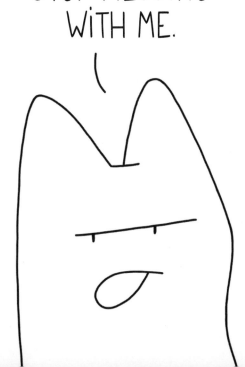

STOP MESSING
WITH ME.

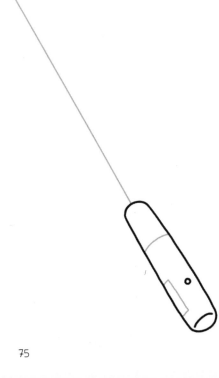

Catsass meets celebrity cats

People say you look like me.
That's embarrassing.

SIMON'S CAT

So no one's noticed
you're evil yet?

CHOUPETTE
LAGERFELD

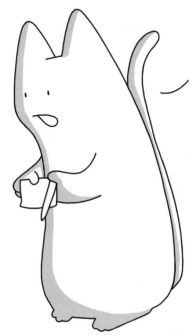

I'm a huge fan of your work. Can I have an autograph?

GRUMPY CAT

Say something, for god's sake!

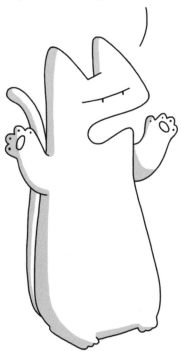

TOM THE CAT

In case you were considering bringing your cat to parties to attract girls . . .

CATSASS FASHION POLICE

Oh, yeah, nice glasses. They really take the attention off your face.

You forgot your pants, miss.

You should wear sandals and socks. Maybe then we'd forget about your terrible outfit.

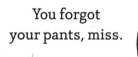

DRESS THE HUMANS UP!

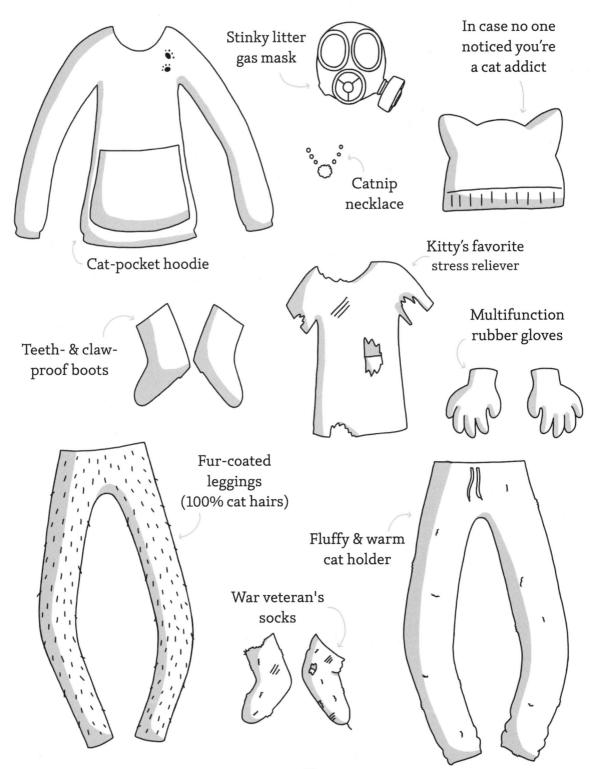

Stinky litter gas mask

In case no one noticed you're a cat addict

Catnip necklace

Cat-pocket hoodie

Kitty's favorite stress reliever

Teeth- & claw-proof boots

Multifunction rubber gloves

Fur-coated leggings (100% cat hairs)

Fluffy & warm cat holder

War veteran's socks

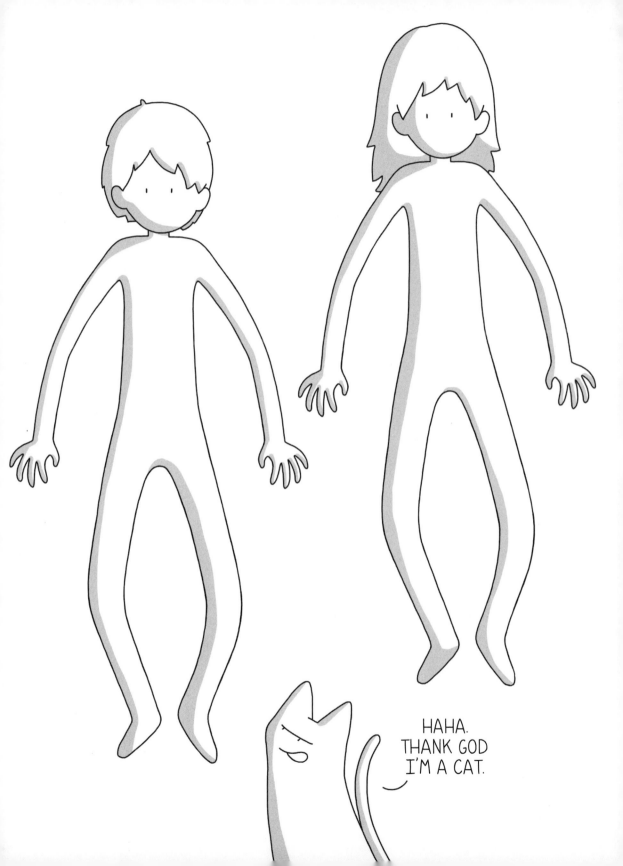

NOW IT'S KITTY'S TURN!

Super cute ear bow

Cool shades

I WILL FUCKING KILL YOU.

Tail pom-pom

Kitty socks

Classy diamond-studded necklace

Bacon T-shirt.

Badass lion wig

Businessy tie

BACON

Bunny costume

Bumblebee
headband

Sushi-cat outfit

Doll dress

Frog hood

CATS' WEIRD EATING HABITS

I DIDN'T SEE YOU WASH YOUR HANDS.

Dogs are useless... Cats can very well be:

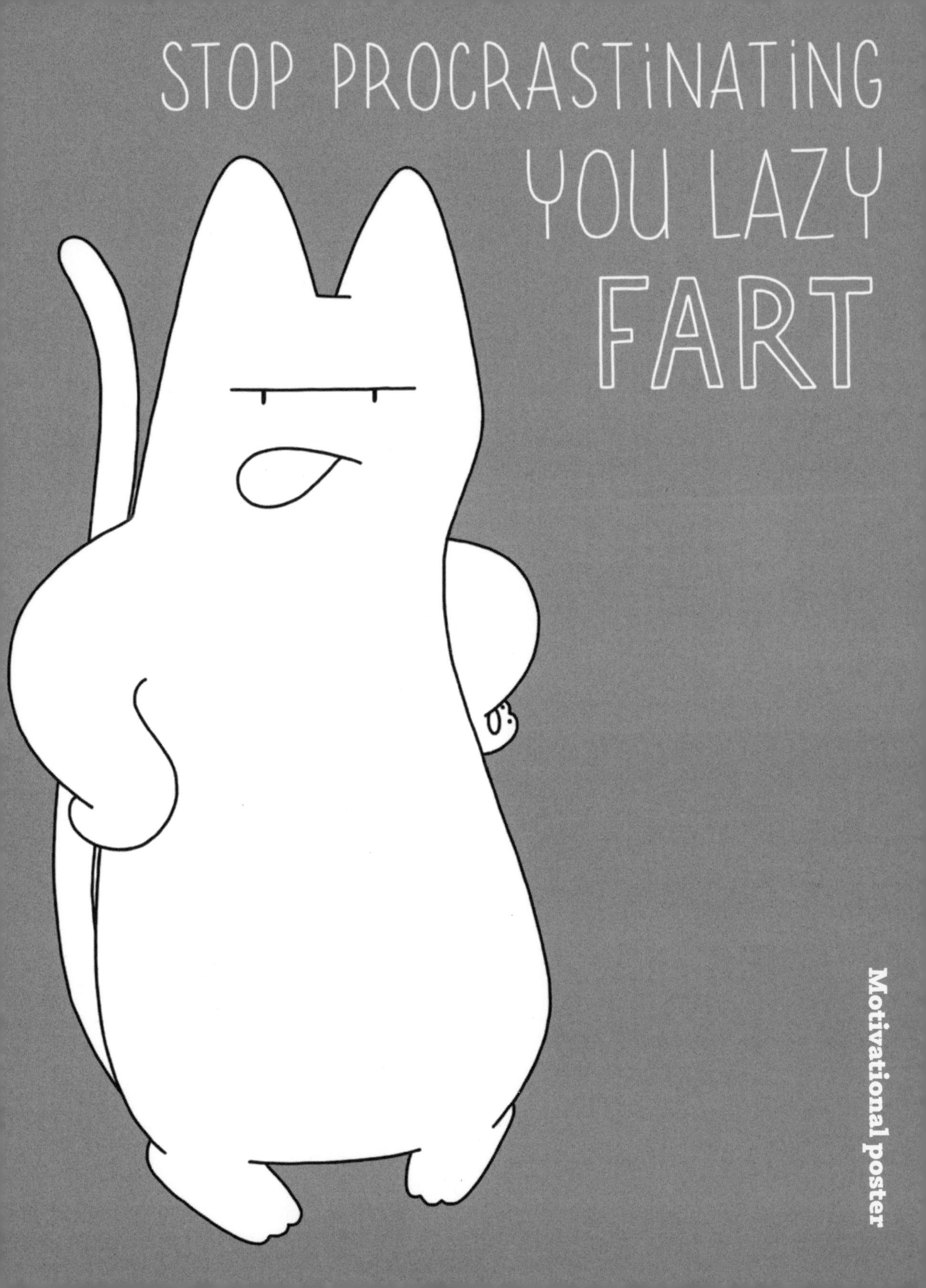
STOP PROCRASTINATING
YOU LAZY
FART
Motivational poster

SUSHI CAT
zen coloring

To all the people who say Catsass is mean, that he's a disgrace to the feline kind:

you just don't get it.

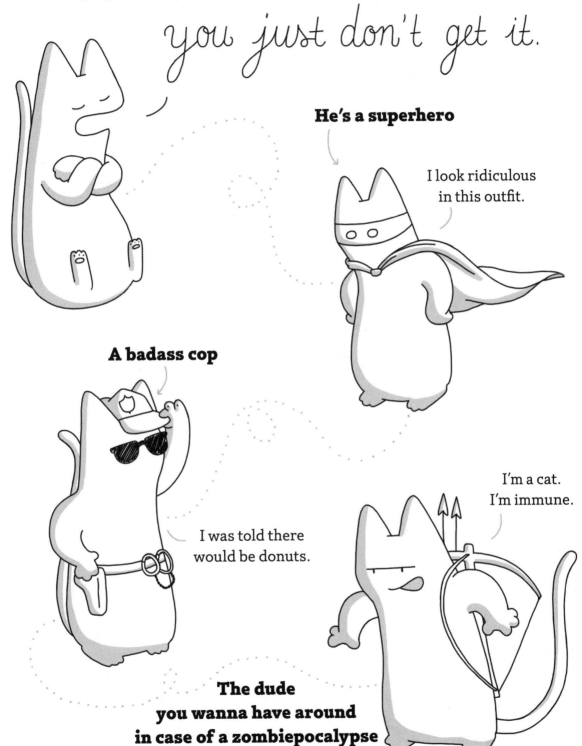

He's a superhero

I look ridiculous
in this outfit.

A badass cop

I was told there
would be donuts.

I'm a cat.
I'm immune.

**The dude
you wanna have around
in case of a zombiepocalypse**

CATSASS HELPS YOU DIET

You sure you wanna eat that?

It highlighted your flabby thighs anyway.

Classic, but it still works every time.

I ate the cheese and the chorizo. Licked a bit of everything, too.

Kitty nail art

Make Catsass's paw look fabulous!

ALWAYS BITE THE HAND THAT FEEDS YOU

Kitty tattoos

That will make you look badass

Cats make great drug smugglers

They look so innocent
no one wants to accuse them

They can't be blamed
for being barked at

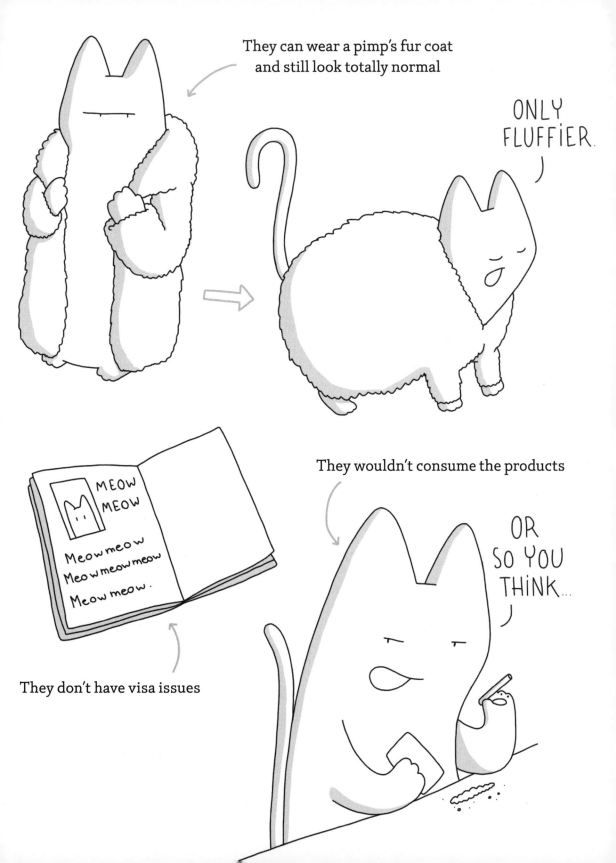

Cat lovers are part of a cult:

They wear a uniform

They try to convert everyone

They spend crazy amounts of money for their gods

They isolate themselves from the rest of the world

YOU WILL CLEAN MY POOP, THEN FEED ME.

YES, MASTER.

They have a well-organized, clear hierarchy

KiTTiiiiES! KiTTiiiES! kiTTiES... KiTTiES...

They have a mantra they repeat all day long

TEST: Are you a real cat?

1 Where do you like to sleep?

a. Anywhere, as long as you can be with the humans.

b. Usually the guest's lap, especially if he's allergic. Sometimes on the bed.

c. Wherever is annoying and uncomforable for others.

2 Your favorite type of food:

a. Anything, really, as long as it's good for your health.

b. Luxury shit. Nothing from the supermarket.

c. Whatever the humans are having. Or maybe something else. Let's just lick it to check.

3 Your friends are . . .

a. Numerous and fantastic!

b. You don't have friends. You have slaves that are sometimes allowed to cuddle you to feel like their life is less empty. Hell is other people.

c. You only have one. Wait, that's your reflection in the mirror.

4) Last time you made a mess, you . . .

a. Hid shamefully under the couch, until you felt forgiven.

b. Stared judgmentally at the human yelling at you, then went to sleep.

c. Enjoyed it. And did it again, three seconds later.

5) If your humans died, you would . . .

a. Weep and visit them every day at the cemetery, until you'd end up on the news.

b. Wonder who is going to feed you. Eat the bodies. Then wonder again.

c. Do your best to erase the fingerprints, hide in Mexico for a while, then find a better, richer family next time.

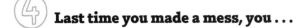

Answers

Mostly a. You, again? You are a fucking dog. Stop pretending.

Mostly b. You're pretty good at what you do. Keep practicing. Soon you'll reach the status of a god.

Mostly c. You're perfect. Stay exactly the way you are. <3

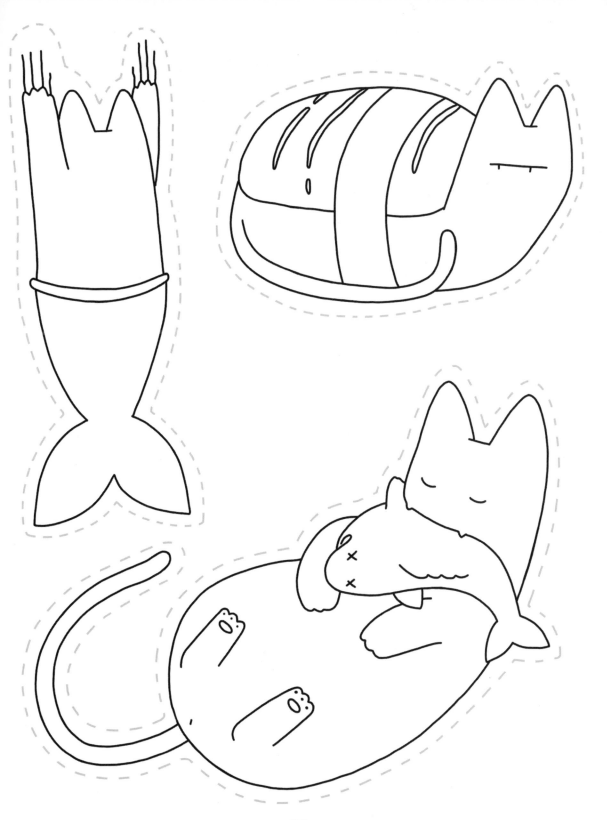

Become a celebrity cat

① Pay a lot of
attention to your looks
(= be cute, or ugly,
or both)

large googly eyes

floppy ears

round fluffy belly

② Develop a skill

play the piano

miaowww...

mew weirdly

be adorably awful

③ Miscalculate your moves

fig. 1   fig. 2   fig. 3

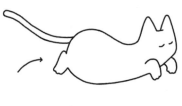

Dear neighbors,

I'm throwing a party at my place on the ....

It's going to be messy and crowded as hell, but given that:

☐ You never recycle

☐ I hear you having sex

☐ I don't like your doormat

☐ It sounds like you're training a soccer team made of elephants

☐ The whole building can tell what you're cooking for dinner
(and you never invite us)

☐ The music you listen to all day long makes me want to rip my ears off

☐ Your face is stupid

I really, REALLY don't care what you think.

(And don't bother knocking on my door, I won't answer.)

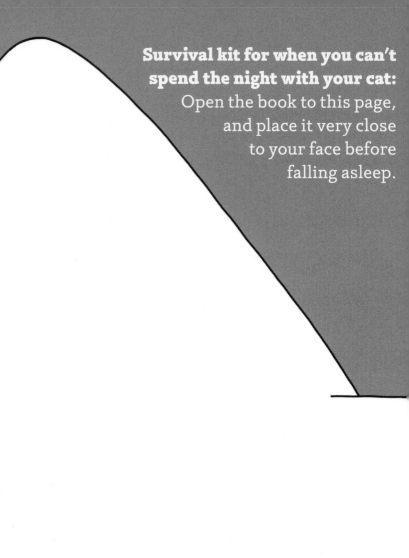

Survival kit for when you can't spend the night with your cat: Open the book to this page, and place it very close to your face before falling asleep.

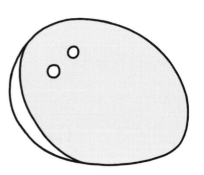

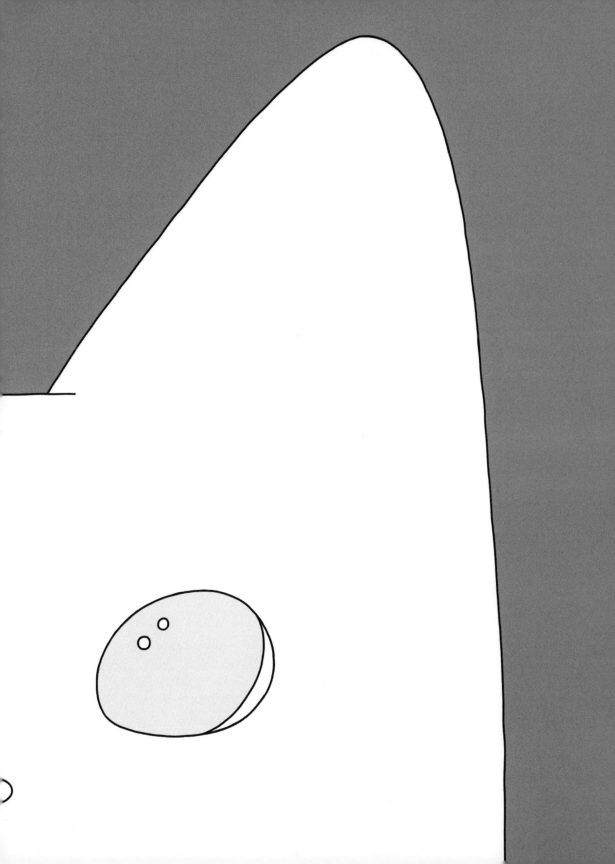

Cat food pyramid

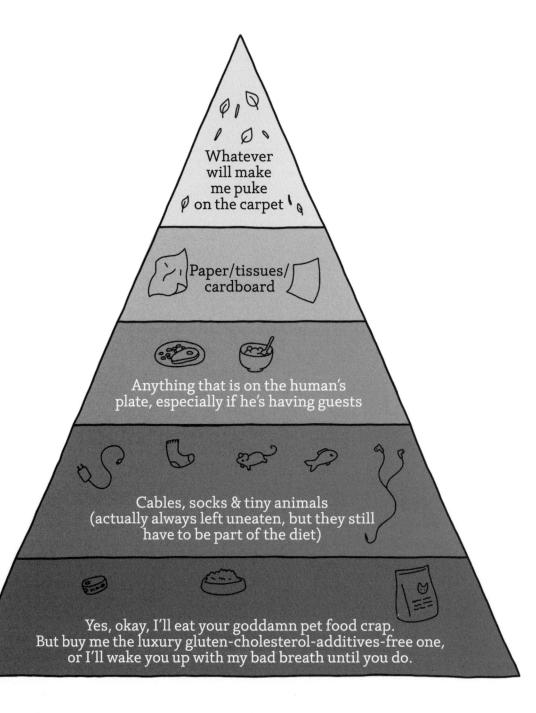

Whatever will make me puke on the carpet

Paper/tissues/cardboard

Anything that is on the human's plate, especially if he's having guests

Cables, socks & tiny animals
(actually always left uneaten, but they still have to be part of the diet)

Yes, okay, I'll eat your goddamn pet food crap.
But buy me the luxury gluten-cholesterol-additives-free one,
or I'll wake you up with my bad breath until you do.

110

DUMBNESS DETECTOR

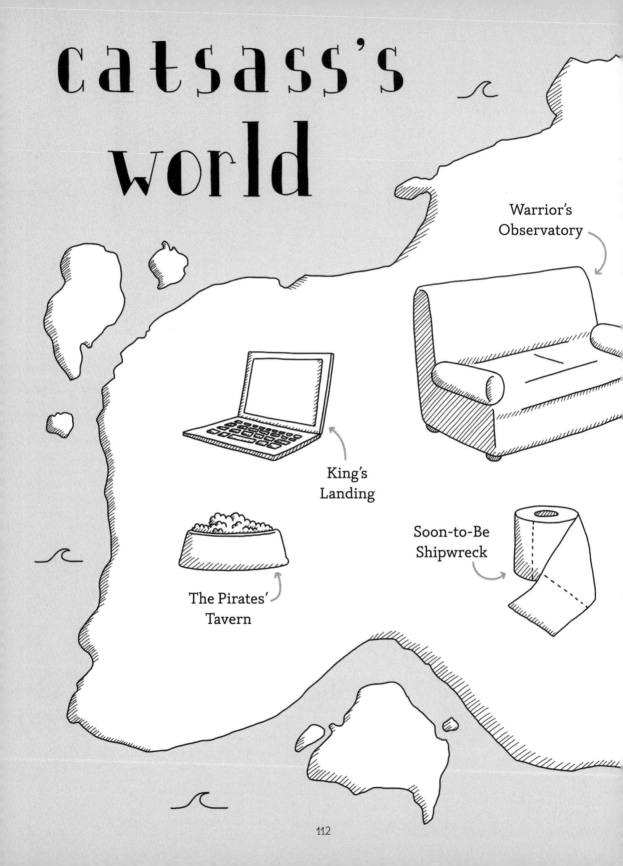

catsass's world

Warrior's
Observatory

King's
Landing

Soon-to-Be
Shipwreck

The Pirates'
Tavern

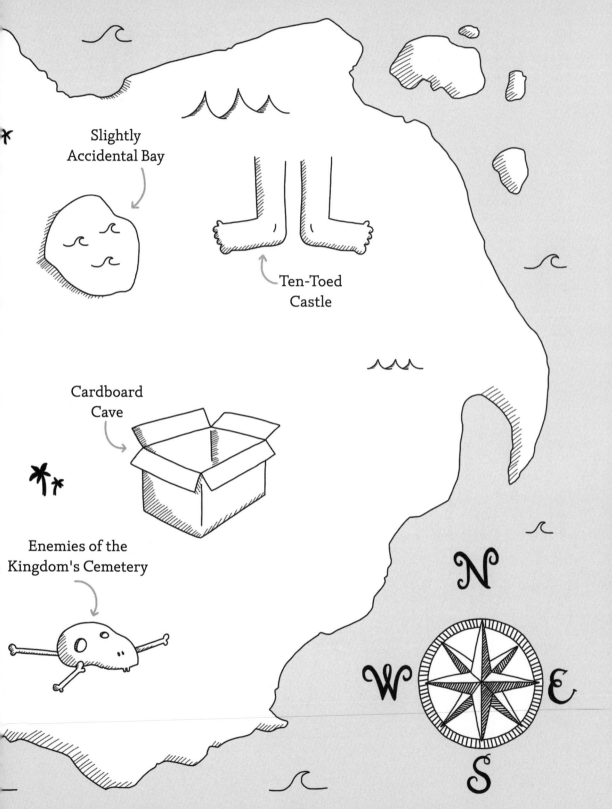

Slightly
Accidental Bay

Ten-Toed
Castle

Cardboard
Cave

Enemies of the
Kingdom's Cemetery

N
W E
S

INTERNATIONAL MEWING

Did you know?

Stray cats don't mew to communicate.
It's a mechanism domestic cats
have developed
to "talk" with humans.

So _yes_, it's just
a way of saying:

FUCK YOU, I WOULDN'T
MAKE THAT SOUND IF
IT WASN'T BOTHERING YOU
SO MUCH.

Cut along the
black lines

Fold along
the dotted
lines

MAKE YOUR OWN

Glue it together

Kitty palace!

**(So yeah, it's just a box.
But man, what a box!)**

Make it look pretty!

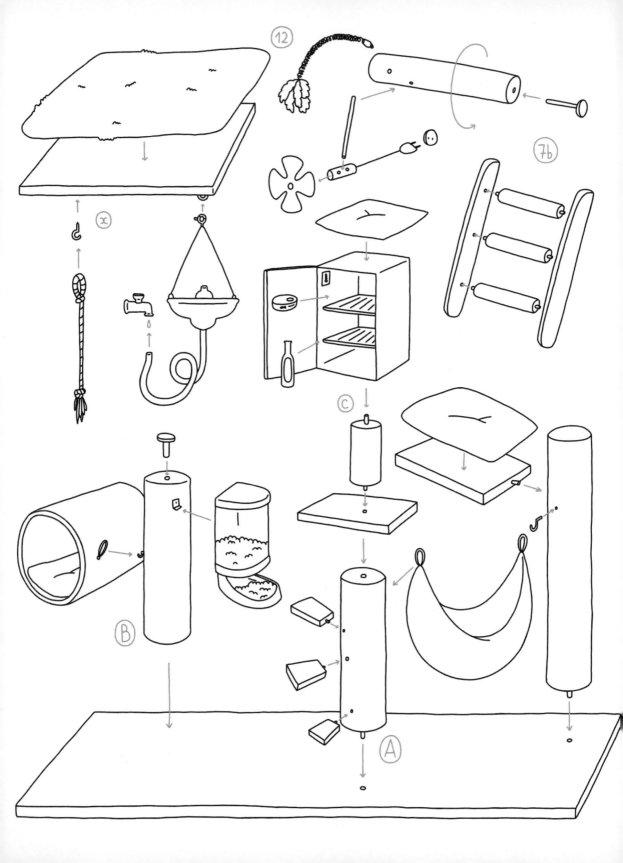

CAT TREE ASSEMBLY INSTRUCTIONS

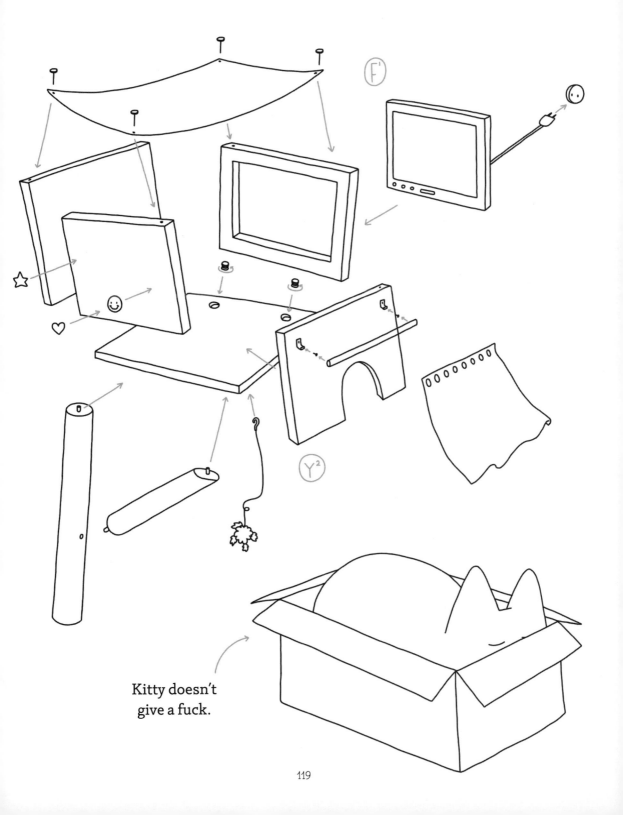

Kitty doesn't give a fuck.

The real explanation of why dinosaurs disappeared

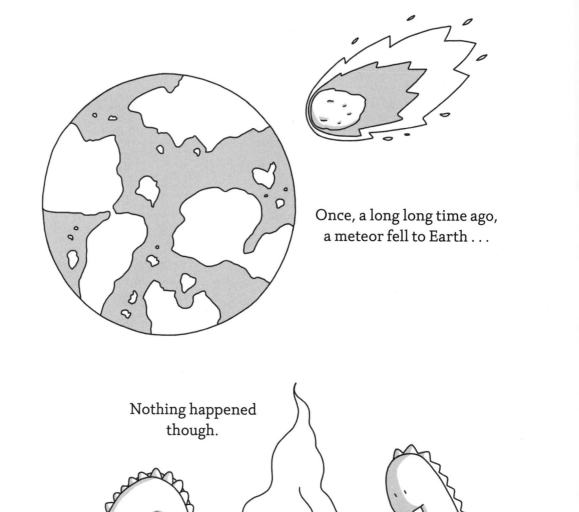

Once, a long long time ago,
a meteor fell to Earth . . .

Nothing happened
though.

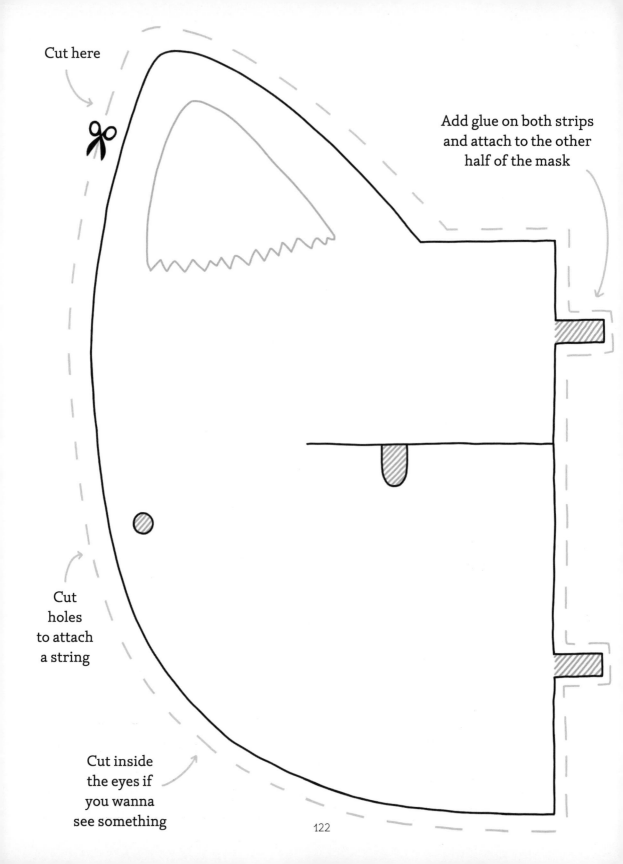

Cut here

Add glue on both strips
and attach to the other
half of the mask

Cut
holes
to attach
a string

Cut inside
the eyes if
you wanna
see something

122

CATSASS MASK!

⬇

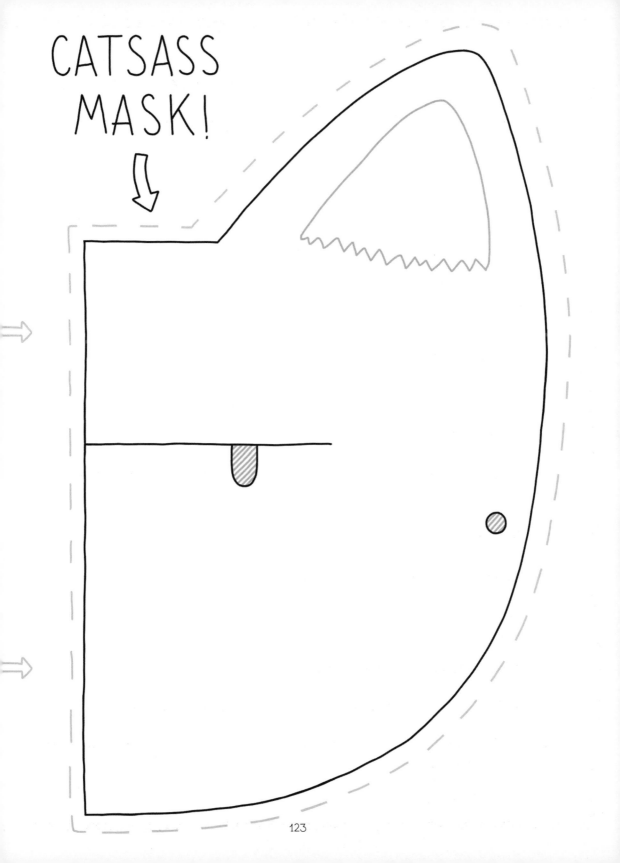

TEST: What will you be reincarnated as?

1) How do you lead your life?

a. You try to help others and be nice to everyone.

b. You are very good at calculating how much work you'll have to do to get others to do what you need them to.

c. You deal with your own problems, fuck the rest. What difference does it make anyway?

2) Are you religious?

a. You believe there's a higher power, and it gives you values of love and respect.

b. Yes. I am God.

c. Religion is the opium of the people.

3) Do you remember your past lives?

a. Well, no, so you're thinking of going to a psychic to help you remember.

b. Yes! They were great. You would go for a walk, eat, and then rub your ass on the floor. Wait . . . that was this morning!

c. You were a cat, obviously.

④ If you ever hurt someone, what will you do?

a. Apologize to him and very likely hurt yourself equally.

b. Put your claws on his thighs, to give him a sense of proportion.

c. Maybe laugh. Probably stare at him judgmentally and leave.

⑤ What would you like to be reincarnated as, if you had the choice?

a. Anything, really. Every living thing is worth being considered.

b. A cat, of course.

c. You probably deserve to be some sort of demigod but don't believe this reincarnation crap.

Answers

Mostly a. You're being such a good person, you'll probably be reborn as a cat. Grow a pair, though. You're about to become a fucking cat.

Mostly b. Obviously, you're already a cat. You'll probably be the same next time, as you've reached perfection.

Mostly c. Seriously, dude. Even in my cat's mind, that's messed up. Reincarnate into a plant or something.

WRITING EXERCISE :
Learn how to mew UNSTOPPABLY

maw maw maw maw maw maw maw
maw maw

AND FiNALLY UNDERSTAND WHAT FEELS SO GOOD ABOUT iT.

CAT BINGO

**What do you come across when visiting a house with cats?
See if you check all the boxes.**

The allergic

The spilled cat food

The cat pics everywhere

The ruined toilet paper

A dead mouse

4 a.m. meowing

MAWMAW MAW MAWMAW MAWMAW MAWMAW MAWMAW MAWMAW

The taken spot

The crazy cat lady

A missing sock

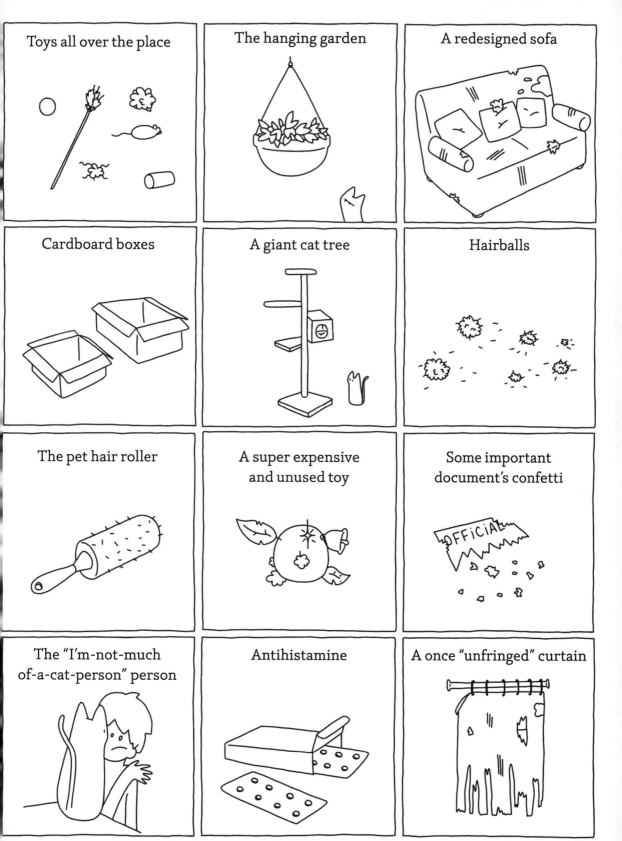

CATS

Censoring humans for 2.8 million years.

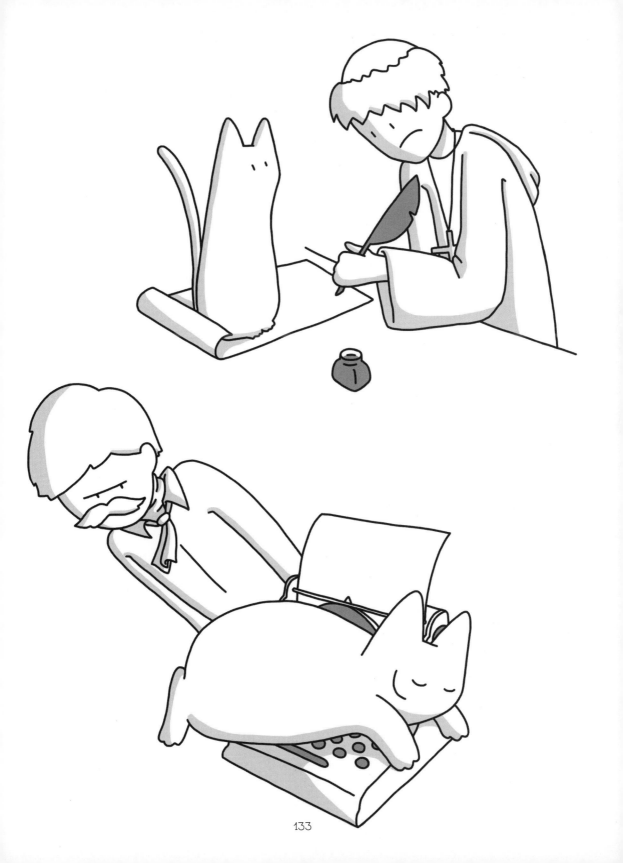

The cat has destroyed most of the socks. Only one pair is still matching. Find it!

TOXOPLASMA GONDii

Or why you still love your cat to bits even though he's an asshole

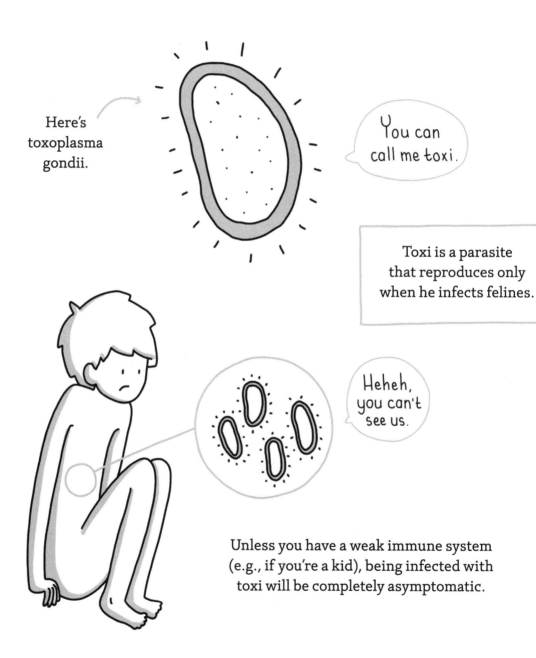

Here's toxoplasma gondii.

You can call me toxi.

Toxi is a parasite that reproduces only when he infects felines.

Heheh, you can't see us.

Unless you have a weak immune system (e.g., if you're a kid), being infected with toxi will be completely asymptomatic.

BUT

Very serious scientific studies proved that infected bodies showed behavioral changes.

Basically, rodents don't fear cats once infected.

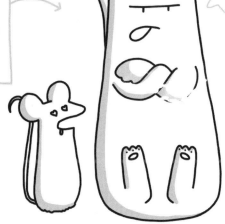

Seriously guys. Get your shit together.

+ SIDE:

You now have a medical excuse to be late for cuddling your cat.

Works the same way for humans . . .

My doctor says there's no cure...

Leave me alone, you crazy germ bag!

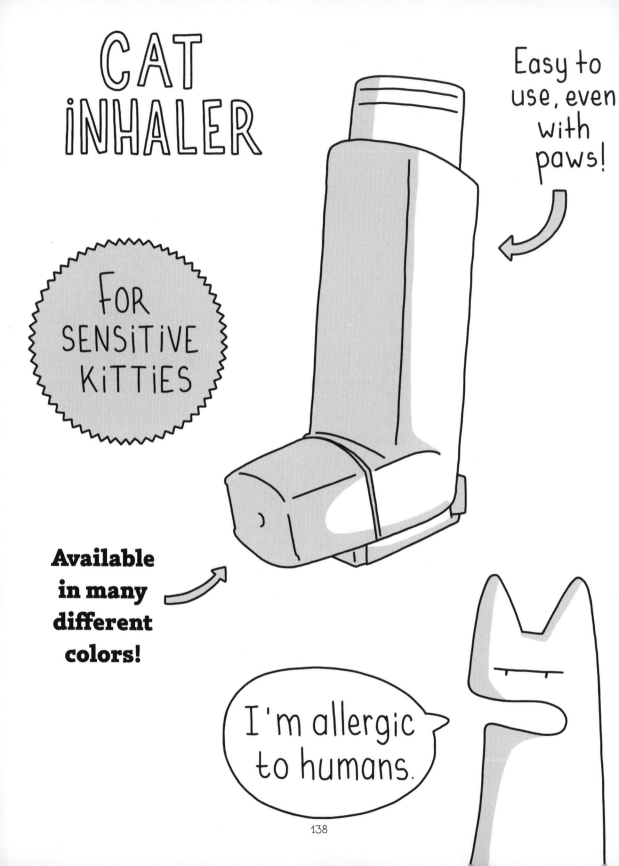

Welcome message

Cut it out & stick it on your door/desk/self

GAMES YOU CAN'T PLAY WITH YOUR CAT

Jenga

Soccer

Hide-and-seek

You can't see meeee . . .

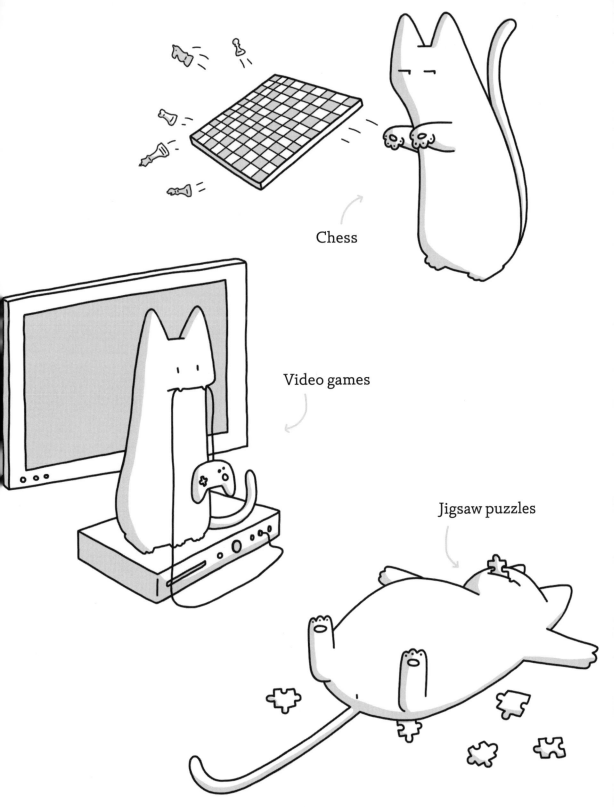

Chess

Video games

Jigsaw puzzles

WAYS TO PASS THE TIME WHEN YOU'RE A CAT:

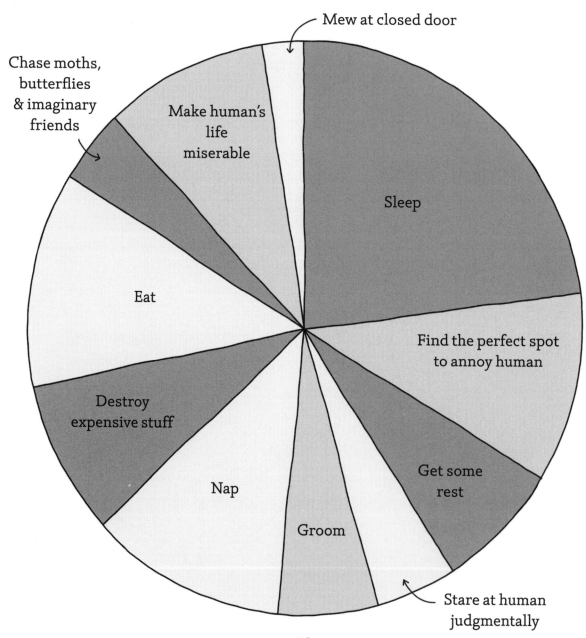

Mew at closed door

Chase moths, butterflies & imaginary friends

Make human's life miserable

Sleep

Eat

Find the perfect spot to annoy human

Destroy expensive stuff

Get some rest

Nap

Groom

Stare at human judgmentally

Cats. Sending messages to space since computers were invented.

Decipher the code and find out what your cat is saying!

A B C D E F G H I J K L M

: H É r 1 $ C q À w Œ U Z

N O P Q R S T U V W X Y Z

(A M y - G I ê % L S 5 †

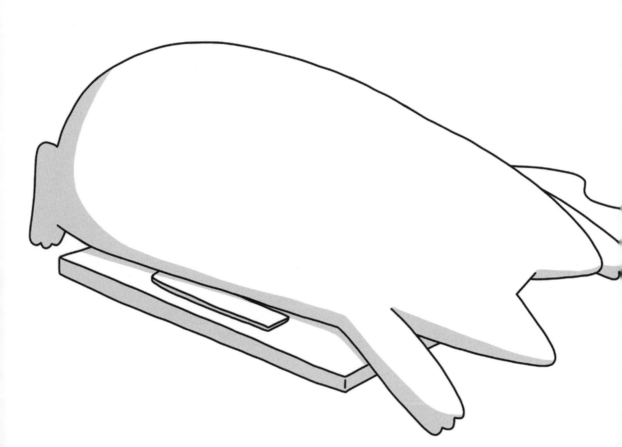

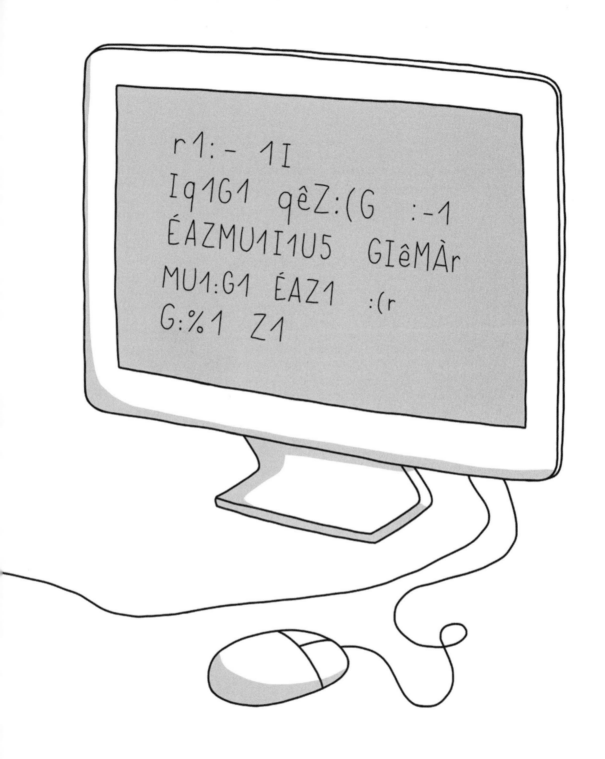

Answer: Dear green thingy, please take me away with you, these humans are so dumb they can't even understand what "meow" means. Don't bother invading this planet—they ruined it.

Ladies and gentlemen, welcome to

PURRY AiRLiNES!

**We remind you that this is
a nonsmoking flight. Smoking is
prohibited on the entire aircraft.**

What am I
gonna doooo?

Dude, you don't
even smoke.

Oh, right.

**In the event of
a loss of cabin pressure,
an oxygen mask
will automatically
appear in front of you.**

Really?
I can't get proper
food, even in
business
class??

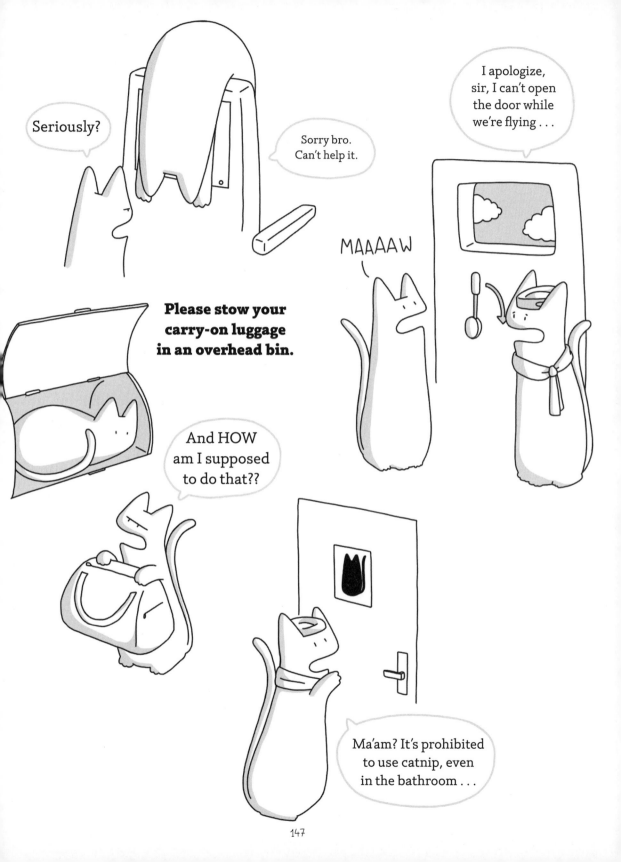

FIND YOUR STUFF

Kitty made a mess! Find the missing sock, a half-eaten cookie, your car keys, your phone charger, the last toilet roll, and your dignity (nevermind, that one left forever when you got a cat).

SPOT THE DIFFERENCE!

CATS ARE WARRiORS

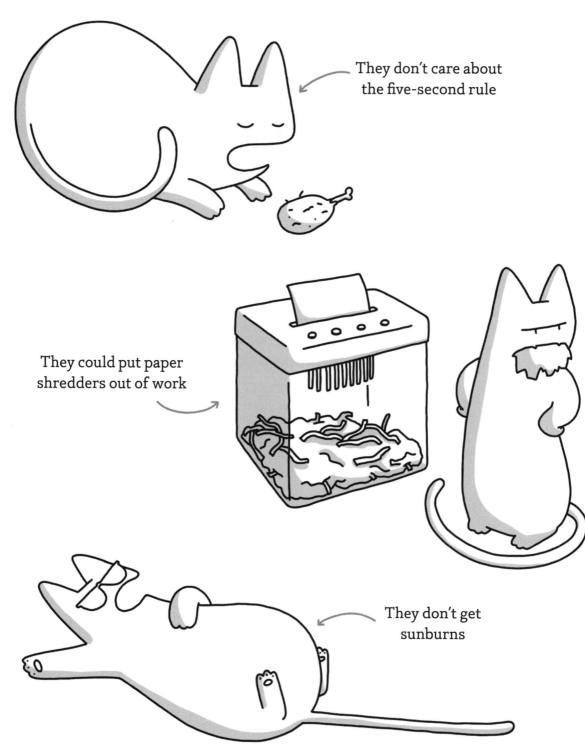

They don't care about
the five-second rule

They could put paper
shredders out of work

They don't get
sunburns

They don't have
to do the dishes

No.

You'd
probably
be super
attractive
if you looked
different.

Also, you smell
like you farted
your soul.

They're so
unquestionably cute
they can say whatever
they want

KITTY MYSTERY RESTAURANT CUSTOMER

What do you mean, "vegetarian"? Do I look like a rabbit?

BEFORE

AFTER

Aren't we supposed to have food with all that decorative salad?

Plus side: The food looks more or less the same after being eaten, digested, and thrown up.

What to do in a heat wave

Tiles are known
to stay cool when it's hot.
Lay on the floor,
preferably in front of a door.

Make your own kiddie pool.

Chill in the fridge. Leave the door open. You don't want to freeze to death in there.

Get a slave to fan you.

Life Lessons from Catsass copyright © 2017 by Claude Combacau.
All rights reserved. Printed in China. No part of this book may be used
or reproduced in any manner whatsoever without written permission
except in the case of reprints in the context of reviews.

Andrews McMeel Publishing
a division of Andrews McMeel Universal
1130 Walnut Street, Kansas City, Missouri 64106

www.andrewsmcmeel.com

17 18 19 20 21 RLP 10 9 8 7 6 5 4 3 2 1

ISBN: 978-1-4494-8528-3

Library of Congress Control Number: 2016962983

Life Lessons from Catsass was first published in
Spain in 2016 by Editorial Planeta.

Editor: Patty Rice
Art Director: Julie Barnes
Production Editor: Erika Kuster
Production Manager: Tamara Haus

ATTENTION: SCHOOLS AND BUSINESSES
Andrews McMeel books are available at quantity discounts with
bulk purchase for educational, business, or sales promotional use.
For information, please e-mail the Andrews McMeel Publishing
Special Sales Department: specialsales@amuniversal.com.